Burmese Pythons

A Pet Guide for Burmese Pythons

Burmese Pythons General Info, Purchasing, Care, Cost, Keeping, Health, Supplies, Food, Breeding and More Included!

By Lolly Brown

Foreword

Burmese pythons are undoubtedly one of the largest snake species in the world. These beautiful yet quite notorious slimy creatures have a reputation for being a quite creative predator. The way Burmese Pythons catch their prey is very different from most snake species, what they do is they use their sharp teeth in order to seize their poor prey, they sink in its rearward pointy teeth and immediately coils its slimy body before actually squeezing it, needless to say, the Burmese Python kills its prey the slow and hard way! After suffocating the animal to death, they then swallow it whole through their flexible jaws that can gobble up five times the size of their head.

Burmese pythons in the wild they mostly would eat anything smaller than them but would also be up for the challenge of eating other larger prey. These creatures are also known for attacking and swallowing large and wild alligators. Despite of their poor vision, these animals can accurately pinpoint where their potential prey is or threat because of their high stalking and preying skills thanks to their tongue receptors and powerful jaws! Do you think you can handle this?

Table of Contents

Introduction

The artfully patterned appearance of the Burmese pythons and its friendly disposition is the reasons why most people get attracted to it and chooses to take care of it as pets despite of some people calling it as one of the dangerous snake species found in the wild. The Burmese python is definitely one of the fastest growing python species in the world, unfortunately most of these docile snakes aren't taken care of properly which is why most of them are just released into the wild.

The Burmese python inhabits mostly grassy marshes and forests in Southeast Asia. They are definitely one of the longest and heaviest snake species on earth so if you're up for a real heavyweight challenge then you might just get served as these snakes can grow up to 25 feet long with a weight of about 200 pounds. They are among the fastest species to mature both in size and "snake abilities." And although they are mostly ground – dwellers, they're also reputable reptile swimmers because they can stay under water for about half an hour. Move over Phelps!

In the United States, Burmese pythons sort of became an attraction mostly for educational or hunting purposes, you can find many reptile enthusiasts and zoologists constantly visiting the famous home of the Burmese pythons in Everglades Park found in Florida USA. There are thousands of these creatures roaming around the area varying in shape, sizes and personality. Some are wild, some are released from captivity so if you're planning to go out there for a hunt make sure that you bring an expert to come with you.

Most of these animals are at very high risk of being endangered because their natural habitat is being depleted, while some of it is illegally traded. Most of these Burmese pythons are also killed for their meat and scales in most countries in Southeast Asia, which is why they have a "vulnerable" status according to IUCN. So make sure that before you acquire one, you've set your mind in being committed and responsible pet owners.

Chapter One: The Burmese Python Species

The population of Burmese pythons is suffering from many factors such as habitat loss due to increased human population as well as illegal trading. These amazing pets are also hunted in the wild for their skins which are then use to turn into leather – based accessories, not to mention they are also killed for their meat especially in their native land in Southeast Asia. These are some of the reasons why in the United States, Burmese pythons are being rescued and taken care of as pets, they are slowly becoming an endangered species and because of that, responsible ownership is being taught by potential pet keepers. In this chapter you will receive an introduction to the breed including some basic biological facts and its physical features.

Taxonomy, Origin and Distribution

Burmese Pythons have a scientific name of *Python molurus bivittatus*. They belong in Kingdom *Animalia*, Phylum *Chordata*, Class *Reptilia*, Order *Squamata*, Family *Boidae*, Genus *Python molorus*, and Species *bivittatus*.

The Burmese pythons are also called as Asiatic Rock Pythons and sometimes Tiger Pythons. These snakes are native in many countries in Asia and Southeast Asia including Pakistan, Eastern India, Nepal, Srilanka, Indonesia, China (southern area), Burma, Celeb Islands, Borneo, Sumatra, Bhutan, Bangladesh, Laos, Vietnam, Myanmar, Cambodia, Thailand, Bali, Sumbawa and Java except the Philippines. They are mostly found in dry jungles, mountains, grasslands, grassy marshes and sometimes in rivers, rocky foothills, valleys, and swamps.

Burmese Python Overview

Burmese pythons as mentioned earlier as undoubtedly one of the heaviest and longest snake species in the world and they are also non – venomous making them ideal as pets. They grow rapidly especially if they live in the wild. Their skin color is dark brown coupled with spots of beige resembling a puzzle piece or skin patterns found in a giraffe (which is why people in the leather manufacturing industry are coming after them). They can also be distinguished by the 2 lines that run on their heads just across both of their eyes. The average adult size is 15 to 20 feet or 5 to 6 meters, hatchlings and juveniles usually reach up to 24 inches or 60 centimeters or more. The average weight for an adult Burmese python is 200 pounds or 90 kilograms!

In the wild, these snakes prey on different mammals, reptiles (big or small) as well as birds. They are also notorious for eating huge mammals like deer and pigs. In captivity, they are being fed with rats and thawed animal meat (more on this in the next few chapters).

Incubation for Burmese python eggs would take about 60 – 80 days (2 – 3 months) depending on the environmental condition. Most pythons including the Burmese python shows rather a much better parental care compared to other reptile species because they incubate the eggs they lay using their own muscle to generate heat. Now that's a motherly love right there! The average eggs laid can reach 100 or more. They become sexually matured at around 3 years of age. Their lifespan is quite long especially if they live in the wild; on average they live for about 20 - 25 years. In fact, the longest living Burmese python ever recorded lasted for 28 years and nearly 3 months.

These pets are listed in the Appendix II of the CITES and labeled as Vulnerable or (have risk of being endangered) by other organizations including the IUCN.

Burmese Python Features

Surface Characteristics:

- Has skin patterns that can camouflage into any grassy or forestry environment.
- Has a skin blotch that makes good leather – based accessories particularly the females (making them more at risk for being hunted).
- Has smooth silky skin and scales

Vestigial Legs Characteristics:

- Has snake spurs and bumps, which are according to scientists, a remnant of their evolutionary history. Scientists believed that pythons are walking reptile creatures.
- The spurs are now used by male Burmese pythons to stimulate their female counterparts.

Coiling Abilities

- Coiling is used to slowly kill their prey until such species suffocates before swallowing it with their flexible and powerful jaws since they are non – venomous.
- The other reason why they coil up is to generate heat for their eggs to keep it warm and incubated. However, the risk here is that the mother python can lose weight during nesting.

Stretchable Skull and Vampire – like Teeth

- The lower jaws of Burmese pythons can open up independently enabling them to fully swallow their prey. Other reptile species do not have this flexible ability.
- They can swallow a prey that is about 5 times the size of their head.
- Their extremely sharp teeth are not built for chewing but rather for puncturing. It is faced backward compared to other snake species.

Eating Habits

- Burmese pythons eat once in a while but of course when they do it's already good for many weeks as they like to eat something that is almost half their body size.

- It takes about 5 - 10 days in digesting their food depending on how big their meal. However, during this digesting time, the Burmese python is motionless.

Quick Facts

Distribution and Range: Pakistan, Eastern India, Nepal, Srilanka, Indonesia, China (southern area), Burma, Celeb Islands, Borneo, Sumatra, Bhutan, Bangladesh, Laos, Vietnam, Myanmar, Cambodia, Thailand, Bali, Sumbawa and Java.

Breed Size: long, heavy, and large – size breed

Body Type and Appearance: Their skin color is dark brown coupled with spots of beige; they can also be distinguished by the 2 lines that run on their heads just across both of their eyes. It has skin patterns that can camouflage into any grassy or forestry environment; has smooth silky skin and scales and the lower jaws of Burmese pythons can open up independently enabling them to fully swallow their prey. **Length and Weight:** The average adult size is 15 to 20 feet or 5 to 6 meters, hatchlings, and juveniles usually reach up to 24 inches or 60 centimeters or more. The average weight for an adult Burmese python is 200 pounds or 90 kilograms!

Skin Texture: scaly with spurs but silky smooth texture

Color: dark brown or beige with blotches

Temperament: docile and non – venomous but can be aggressive when threatened.

Diet: Burmese pythons feed on birds, rats, deer, rabbits, pigs, squirrel, and mostly wild mammals found in the forest as well as reptile species like the American alligator.

Habitat: They are mostly found in dry jungles, mountains, grasslands, grassy marshes and sometimes in rivers, rocky foothills, valleys, and swamps.

Health Conditions: generally healthy but predisposed to common illnesses such as IBD (Inclusion Body Disease), Stomatitis or Mouth Rot, Parasitism, Rectal Prolapse, Tail – Hanging, Lung Infections, Dermatitis, and Toxemia

Lifespan: On average they live for about 20 - 25 years. The longest living Burmese python ever recorded lasted for 28 years and nearly 3 months.

Chapter Two: What Makes Burmese Pythons Ideal as Pets

The real question is, are you also an ideal pet Burmese python keeper? In this chapter, we will delve deeper on what it takes to really become a keeper by learning about its temperament as well as the license or permit needed for keeping them, and also the budget you'll most probably need to provide all its requirements. These are all important before you purchase a Burmese python snake as your pet. You as a potential keeper need to make sure that your pet snake is safe, secure, and happy.

Tips Before Bringing a Burmese Pet Home

Burmese Pythons are being rumored as a "deadly" snake species because according to some people these snakes have attacked their owners before and hunters are being eaten alive in the wild. Some people say that those stories are only myths, and while it's true that these snake species are very powerful and can definitely kill a human, it shouldn't be something that is totally fenced off from those who wanted to keep them as pets especially now that these animals are slowly becoming vulnerable.

Do you have what it takes?

The Burmese Python may not be ideal as pets if you're a first time snake keeper or python keeper for that matter as they can be quite a lot to handle not to mention their habitat maintenance since they can reach their maximum size in just a few years. Here are some questions to ask yourself before getting a Burmese Python as pets:

- Do you have enough knowledge and experience in handling or keeping snakes?
- Can you provide an adequate living condition for them?
- Can you take the time to learn how to take care of

them from hatchlings until they reach adulthood?

- Can you afford to buy everything they need including its diet, cage or enclosures, permits, habitat maintenance materials, veterinary expenses in cases of medical emergencies etc?
- Can you handle the breeding process and breeding maintenance of your snake if ever you decided to breed them?
- Can you handle bites from time to time? All snake keepers even if their pet is docile still get bitten every now and then – it's part of the job, do you think you can handle that?
- Are your friends and family okay with keeping a snake as pets?

Does Your Housemates Have What It Takes?

Speaking of friends and family, one of the biggest hurdles to getting a pet snake is convincing your housemates. Obviously, the idea of keeping a snake at home is not common, and to one who is not used to snakes, having one at home can be terrifying especially if they have a phobia of snakes.

In this section, we will give you some tips on how to persuade anyone in your house to let you have a pet snake and assure them that it is safe and family – friendly so to speak:

Do's

- Familiarize your housemates about the snake first. Introduce it to them and tell them about its biological background or tell stories of how pet owners are having fun taking care of them so that they can get used to the idea of it.
- Answer their questions about Burmese pythons like the benefits of taking care of one, how much it will cost, and how big it will get.
- Be honest so that they will be able to assess the risks and costs of living with a pet snake.
- Show them how easy it is to maintain and take care of a Burmese python
- Share stories about how other owners are having fun keeping snakes as pets so your family or friends will know that they do not have to be afraid.
- Assure your relatives or housemates that you are responsible enough to keep your snake, and that they won't end up having to feed it for you or fight it off, if it escapes and becomes agitated. This can only be done by showing them, not just telling them, that you are a responsible keeper.

Don'ts

- Never tell your family out of nowhere that you already bought or acquired a pet snake without consulting them first (this is a no – brainer).

- Don't force your family or housemates about keeping a Burmese python if they seriously don't want to even if you've done everything to inform or educate them. The snake might get stressed and/or agitated because they can smell fear from a mile away.

- If they don't want it, don't push it! Learn to wait until you can get your own place or until you have their approval. Before you get your own Burmese python, you must make sure the people you live with are okay with it, if you can't find anyone willing to support you either your roommates or family members, it is better not to take care of one at least in the meantime. Otherwise, you might end up having to relocate it and snakes aren't easy to put up for adoption or just give to anyone.

Do you have what it takes to keep more than one Burmese Snake?

Just like when considering other pets, the decision of whether you can keep more than one Burmese Python or not depends on your overall capacity to commit to all of them.

Of course, you must also keep in mind that keeping more than one pet means an increase in responsibility and concerns – financially, time wise, and even mentally. Efforts of cleanup and cage maintenance will be doubled, or tripled, if you're feeling quite up for it. So before committing to buying more than one, you should objectively assess your capacity to provide what your pets will require otherwise you could end up just releasing them into the wild.

Preparation and readiness is key so make sure to make an informed and responsible decision on how many Burmese Pythons you can responsibly and dutifully care for and keep.

Burmese Python Temperament

As one of the friendly python species, Burmese pythons are docile, non – venomous and can adapt with human contact especially if they are being handled at an early age. Their non – venomous and also non – aggressive nature makes them ideal as family pets even if you have kids.

If you get to handle them, what they usually do is they'll coil up either on your hand or your body (if they are quite long already) and flicker their tongue to sort of "assess" you. If you have children of course, it's always good to not left them unsupervised with the snake. Make sure that the snake is also comfortable with being handled before actually handing them out to your kids.

Keep in mind that these snakes are still animals at the end of the day, even if they're docile and used to interacting with humans it's still advisable to be cautious all the time especially when handling and feeding them.

Can Burmese Snake Co – Inhabit with Other Household Pets?

Yes and no. That answer depends on how big your shelter or enclosure is since these pets can grow super long over time the issue here won't be about temperament but rather territoriality. If not enough space is adequately provided for them, they might end up attacking each other or competing for space.

In terms of housing them with other household pets, your dog or cat is safe as long as they don't come anywhere near the cage or enclosure of your Burmese python since these animals prey on mammals, it's better to keep your other pets away from the snake to avoid any casualties.

Pros and Cons of Burmese Pythons

Pros

- Burmese Pythons are aesthetically appealing creatures.

- These snakes have a docile and people – friendly temperament.
- Burmese Pythons will surely keep any expert snake keeper on their feet. Maintenance can be quite challenging but also fun.
- These creatures are generally low-key and shy but I'm sure they won't mind you petting them.
- Burmese Pythons live for a very long time as long as you provide its needs and care for it properly. They can live for up to 20 – 25 years or more!
- These snakes are not stinky so you don't have to worry about regularly bathing them.

Cons

- Burmese Pythons does get very long and heavy. If you aren't prepared to handle a 200 pound snake, maybe it's not for you.
- These pets are quite sensitive to temperature and humidity changes, so you would have to be extra careful to make sure that they are comfortable.
- Finding a vet clinic well-equipped enough to treat your Burmese Python can be hard since not all vets are reptile experts.
- If you are out of town for example, it'll be quite hard to find a friend willing to feed your pet since most people are afraid of snakes.

- If you are afraid of handling, petting or even feeding a baby Burmese python, then it's better to not buy this species in particular because it will surely get large and very tough to handle – definitely not for faint – hearted keepers.

Burmese Python Permits/Licensing Reminders

- The Burmese Python is included in Appendix II of the Convention on International Trade in Endangered Species of Wild Fauna and Flora or CITES wherein the international trade involving it is monitored and regulated.

- There is no federal law governing private possession or ownership of exotic animals in the United States.

- You need to pay attention not on a national level but on a local level to see what is permitted and what is not.

- The regulations vary from locale to locale, some states might require you to microchip your pet, proof of an established relationship with a veterinarian, and also pet insurance. Some may also ask you to present proof that you are acquiring the animal from a recognized breeder and that the snake was bred in captivity.

- Consult with local United States Fish and Wildlife Service Office to make sure that you are not breaking any laws.

- Make sure to check the rules about keeping pet snakes based on where you are to avoid penalties or confiscation of your pet. You might not even be able to find a veterinarian willing to give your Burmese Python medical care if you are found to be keeping it without the correct permits.

- Permits may also be necessary for importing, exporting, or traveling with an exotic or a naturally dangerous animal.

- Make sure that you are constantly updated on the information regarding your local state laws at least once every six months. Regulations can change, and so as not to find yourself suddenly in violation of a law.

Cost of Owning a Burmese Python

Keeping pets in general can be costly, and even if these snakes are low maintenance and quite inexpensive compared to other breed, you will still need to provide its supplies to maintain a healthy lifestyle and adequate environment for your pet.

In this section you will receive an overview of the expenses associated with purchasing and keeping snakes as pets such as food, maintenance supplies, enclosures, veterinary care, and other essential costs.

Basic Keeping Materials Checklist

Here are some recommendations of what you need to buy:

Purchase Cost:

- A Burmese Python may cost anywhere from $200 to $500, depending on the type, sex, quality, age, and breeder.
- Some Burmese Pythons with quite rare colorings or skin patterns could be much more expensive than the regular ones.

- The money you would have to spend would not be limited to just the purchase price. You have to consider shipping costs and procurement of necessary permits especially if you are ordering one from an international market.
- Shipping fees start at about $30 and will increase depending on the area of origin and delivery place.

Cage/Enclosure:

- Part of keeping a fast growing snake is the need to buy a huge enclosure to fully accommodate it once it is full - grown.
- The rule of thumb is that they should be able to fully stretch out inside its cage.
- Make sure that you also buy a secure screen top to prevent your pet from escaping.

Substrate/Bedding:

- A substrate which will function as your python's bedding. It's highly recommended that you buy aspen shadings, reptile bar or coconut fiber so that your pet will get easily comfortable with its new habitat.

Cage Accessories:

- Opt to provide a cozy hiding place that is large enough for your pet Burmese to coil up inside whenever he feels like it.

- It's also best to purchase some cage furniture or décor to make the enclosure aesthetically appealing (at least while they're still young and small), although don't put too much so that that your pet can have enough space. Once they reached maturity, it is best not to put any decorations any more as they will just destroy it.

- You should also keep in mind to never put any outdoor stuff because it can harm your pet or may be toxic for them.

- Purchase a relatively large water dish to give your Burmese python a place to soak in. Of course, provide a bigger one once it reaches full adult size.

- You also need to purchase a basking lamp, and an under tank heater as well as gauges to regulate temperature and humidity levels to keep your snake at a proper temperature.

- Opt to buy a separate tank for the purpose having

another enclosure whenever you are cleaning their tank or during feeding time.

Food:

- Burmese Pythons typically eat mice or thawed pinkies while they're still young, but it is recommended that you convert them to eating rats as soon as possible.

- An adult Burmese Python should be fed frozen-thawed food.

Insurances/Veterinary Expenses/Permit Expenses:

- It is a good idea to have your pet insured. It is also wise to always have spare cash handy in case emergencies involving your snake (like if ever they injure somebody).

- You also have to take your pet to the vet for a routine check-up every once in a while to make sure it is healthy.

- You should also take into account the costs of a permit or license, the fees of which are subject to change depending on your state or township laws and regulations. Not to mention the micro-chipping expenses if authorities will recommend it.

Cost of Keeping a Burmese Snake:

- Purchase price: $200 - $500
- Glass Enclosure with a screen top or lid: approx. $100 (depending on size)
- Bedding or Substrate: $10
- Water Dish: $10 - $15 (depending on size/quality)
- Under Tank Heater: $25 or more
- Basking Lamp: $30 or more
- Heat and Water Temperature Regulator/ Gauges: $5 or more (often comes with the under tank heater/basking lamp)
- Hiding Place: $5 - $10
- Feeding tank: $30 - $50 or more
- Food: $10 - $15 (depending on brand and amount)
- Vet bills: $75 or more
- License/Permit: depends on the state/country you live in.

Chapter Three: Purchasing and Selecting a Healthy Breed

If you've finally decided to take care of a Burmese python or perhaps you've already convinced your family to keep one, then the next logical step is to actually buy the snake. This is going to initially be one of the best parts in being a snake keeper or pet keeper for that matter. Some of the basic things you would have to consider before buying a Burmese Python would be to determine the sex, age, and perhaps its initial personality. Do you want a male or female, a mature or a juvenile? It's entirely up to you but you have to know that whatever you choose it has its corresponding responsibility.

Aside from that you should also acquaint yourself with the local breeder from whom you will purchase your pet snake. This chapter will give you a wealth of information on what to know when it comes to picking the right pet and the right breeder for you.

Places Where You Can Buy Burmese Pythons

Finding a Burmese python isn't hard since it's also one of the most popular python breeds among reptile enthusiasts. You can buy it in the following places:

- Large or Major Pet Stores
- Reptile Conventions or Snake Expos
- Private Breeders
- Online Sellers/Pet Stores

I would recommend you to buy directly from the breeder because the major advantage of buying from a private breeder is that you'll be provided with the necessary information about your Burmese python. Such important information includes:

- Bloodline/ Lineage / Family History (for possible disease history/ genetics)

- Husbandry Needs (Temperature, Lighting, Environmental Condition)
- Nutrition (Diet, Food Amount, Frequency)
- Medical History (Vaccines (if any))
- Personality/ Temperament of the Species

However, you should also bear in mind that there are other factors that you need to consider in choosing where to make your purchase. While purchasing directly from a breeder does have its advantages, it's not always true for other snake breeders.

Here are some of the advantages and disadvantages of acquiring a pet snake from private breeders and purchasing from reptile expos:

- Private breeders may charge a lot if they are dealing with a particularly rare or should I say much more aesthetically looking Burmese python.

- Breeders especially large – scale sellers sometimes may charge more because of the huge overhead expense they spent during their breeding process.

- Consulting private breeders sometimes can also add up to the final cost you have to pay, though most of them will happily help you out especially if they're breeding for passion's sake.

- Reptile expos, where reptile and snake enthusiasts often converge, are also a good place to look for people passionate about the animals and would be more than willing to answer questions about the creatures.

- Meeting with people is a good way to gauge if they are actually knowledgeable about a certain species or if they are just trying to make the sale.

- To avoid getting scammed by snake breeders who aren't really snake experts, you should note how confident they are in providing answers to your questions, and how easily they give the information.

- Another advantage of buying from breeders either privately or during reptile expos is that you'll be able to directly get to know them and have the opportunity to build a rapport, since these people may be the ones to help you out should you encounter problems with your Burmese python in the future.

What Kind of Breeder Should You Purchase From?

If you decided to buy from a private breeder and not from pet stores, then it is best that you know the kind of breeder you're going to deal with and if this potential breeder is worth your time and money.

Below are some facts about the two kinds of snake breeders:

Home-based Breeders vs. Business Breeders

- Breeders range from large-scale operations to small-scale, private setups.

- Breeders with large budgets or those who breed for business have legit websites filled with snake facts and official sources, while some home-based breeders have blogs that detail personal accounts of handling snakes and other reptiles.

- Some breeders choose to go to more formal and traditional route by attending reptile expos and showing off their breeds.

- Most home – based business and medium – sized breeders just do their own promotion or even supply pet stores instead of putting up their own store.

Breeder Checklist

Tip #1: Look for snake breeders with good reputation.

Good reputation goes a long way! You can never go wrong if a certain breeder is referred by most people especially if good comments are flooding the breeder's way. Here's how you can find breeders with good reputation:

- Join up online forums and discussions to see which ones are the "big names" in breeding high-quality Burmese python.
- Ask your friends if they know any reputable breeders around.
- Read up articles with good sources.
- Interview snake or python owners to see where they purchase their pets.
- Look out for animal organizations/ wildlife pages that recommend certain breeders or websites near your area.
- Ask a veterinarian if they know any reputable breeders around – if your ideal vet recommended a certain breeder that's already a big advantage because it has approval from your vet.

Tip #2: Know what you want.

If you have a clear idea of what kind of Burmese python you like, it'll be much easier to look for a breeder that would meet the standards of your ideal pet in mind. It will also help limit your search parameters for breeders. Focusing on breeders specializing in Burmese pythons furthermore will save you precious time and energy. You will also be able to ask more relevant questions pertaining to the Burmese pythons.

Tip #3: Look for breeders who are also finding "responsible keepers"

Most breeders will be happily answering beginner questions from fellow enthusiasts, but they will also make sure that you are up for the challenge of caring for the snake especially the Burmese python as this snake is just continuously being released in the wild because the owners were not able to maintain them due to their growing size. A reputable breeder wants to make sure that their pets will be handled by "responsible keepers"

Tip #4: Better to Buy from Breeders near You

It is ideal that you purchase locally than purchase from far - flung places or even other countries. Long distance keeps you from meeting the breeder face-to-face and also hinders you from seeing your intended purchase for yourself. It's much better to meet not just the potential breeder but also the potential breed of Burmese python you'd like to buy.

Tip #5: See Where the Action Happens

If you purchase from nearby reputable breeders, you'll have the opportunity to visit or have a tour of their breeding facilities. This is the major advantage of buying from local breeders because you can see for yourself if their setup is following the right husbandry practices. Visiting the site can also build rapport and an inside connection that you would need when time for actual purchase comes as during the first few weeks of your Burmese python you might find yourself in need of breeder advice.

Signs of a Healthy Burmese Python

Regardless the age, sex, or size of Burmese python you are looking for, the number one thing to keep in mind is to pick a snake with no illnesses or diseases, and as much as possible, no temperamental issues that would make things difficult for you when it comes to general snake husbandry such as feeding or cleaning their cage. Below are the signs of a healthy Burmese Python:

- Has a well-rounded body
- Clean and clear eyes and vent
- There should be no signs of respiratory problems, such as wheezing when held, mouth opening a lot, nasal discharge, and mucus around or large bubbles in the mouth.
- They should also be free of parasites such as ticks and mites.
- In terms of behavior, the Burmese python must be somewhat curious and open to your touch, gripping you when being handled.
- In terms of feeding practices, try to see how they respond to feeding from their breeder so that you'll know if they are picky eaters or would have no problem whatsoever.

Recommended Breeders and Rescue Websites

If you prefer acquiring a Burmese python without the need of interviewing or scouting for reputable breeders then you might also want to consider adoption through rescue organizations. Aside from skipping the hassle of finding a good breeder, you can also somewhat acquire a pet at a much cheaper price since these pets are abandoned by their owners so they're like literally given away for potential pet owners.

Here is the list of breeders and adoption rescue websites around United States and United Kingdom:

United States Breeders and Rescue Websites

Morph Market
<https://www.morphmarket.com/us/c/reptiles/pythons/burmese-pythons>

Back Water Reptiles
<http://www.backwaterreptiles.com/pythons/burmese-python-for-sale.html>

Bob Clark Inc.
<http://www.bobclark.com/available/burmese_pythons/>

Reptile City
<http://www.reptilecity.com/Merchant2/merchant.mvc?Screen=CTGY&Store_Code=reptiles&Category_Code=Python>

Kingsnake
<http://market.kingsnake.com/index.php?cat=7>

Gumtree

<https://www.gumtree.com/pets/uk/burmese+python+for+sale>

Pre - Historic Pets

<http://www.prehistoricpets.com/c/29/burmese>

The Serpentarium Inc.

<http://www.snakemuseum.com/61-pythons>

Twin Cities Reptiles

<https://www.twincitiesreptiles.net/live-stock/snakes/pythons/>

Snakes at Sunset

<http://snakesatsunset.com/snakes-for-sale/>

Reptile Rapture

<http://reptilerapture.net/cb-albino-burmese-python-male.html>

LLL Reptile

<https://www.lllreptile.com/articles/153-burmese-python/>

United Kingdom Breeders and Rescue Websites

Preloved UK
<http://www.preloved.co.uk/classifieds/pets/reptiles/all/uk/burmese+python>

NewsNow UK
<https://www.newsnow.co.uk/classifieds/pets-animals/albino-burmese-python-for-sale.html>

Lincoln Reptile and Pet Centre UK
<http://www.lincolnreptileandpetcentre.co.uk/html/burmese-pythons.html >

Pets 4 Homes UK
<https://www.pets4homes.co.uk/sale/reptiles/python-snake/>

Exotic – Pets UK
<https://www.exotic-pets.co.uk/burmese-python.html>

Mansfield Aquatic, Reptile & Pet Centre
<http://www.marpc.co.uk/html/burmese-pythons.html>

Chapter Four: Habitat Requirements for Burmese Pythons

The natural habitat of Burmese Pythons in the wild is mainly in marshy grasslands, jungles, river valleys, and in rocky foothills. Of course, you won't be able to replicate their habitat in the wild exactly like it is inside the terrarium or enclosure but thanks to many reptile accessories you as the owner can sort of mimic their natural environment right at the comfort of your own home! Other parts of setting up includes lighting, temperature, humidity, and the right cage size and materials so that your pet will happily and comfortably adjust to being captive pets.

Proper Husbandry Needs and Cage Set Up

The terrarium or shelter for your pet should have a wide space that can accommodate not just your pet's growing size but also spatial needs. However, the size should also be just enough to ensure that the humidity levels and temperature can be easily set up. Since Burmese pythons are ground dwelling snakes, you have to make sure that the space of the floor is much larger or wider than the height of the enclosure because they will spend most of their time on the ground unlike other tree – dwelling pythons or snakes.

Young Burmese Python Cage Size

A young Burmese python's ideal cage size is a 10 – gallon tank or terrarium. Of course, the larger the snake, the larger the cage so just adjust accordingly. Since Burmese pythons grow heavier over time, the floor space that they would need should be 4 x 8 (feet). The ground space should be 4 to 6 times larger or wider than your pet if he/she is in a coiled up position.

Make sure that you also provide a door that can be both easily access and can also be tightly secured. What most snake keepers buy is a Plexiglas window so that you can also view your snake and observe it from time to time. You should also take note that ventilation is important. Small vents on the side of the enclosure will allow for proper heat and humidity levels as well as adequate air ventilation.

The enclosure you can buy could be made out of wood, plastic or glass, all of which is acceptable but glass and wood are preferred. Perhaps the main advantage of using plastic as an enclosure is that it can be easily spot cleansed since there are no corners or edges compared to wood or glass terrariums. This decision is entirely up to you and your budget.

Once your snake develops over time, you might need to buy a bigger one to accommodate its growing size or you might want to consider setting up a shelter especially if you're planning to keep more than one Burmese python snake.

Substrate

Substrate or bedding is another important thing you need to cover aside from cage accessories like water dishes/ food dishes and basic heating and lighting equipment (which we will talk about in the next section). The substrate is the second most important thing you need to consider next to setting up the cage size. The substrate will serve as the substitute for soil or ground just like how it is in their natural habitat in the wild. It will also serve as humidifiers inside the cage in order to control the temperature. You can buy different kinds of substrate for your pet at local pet stores. Some common types include the following:

- Woods
- Aspen Shavings
- Shredded products
- Newspaper

Humidity and Temperature Levels

Temperatures in their natural habitat are around 70 – 80 degrees Fahrenheit so to be able to replicate this in a cage means providing supplemental heating sources. Here are some examples of heating sources you can buy at your local pet store:

- Under tank heater
- Basic light bulbs
- Ceramic heat emitters
- Heat Pads (never use hot rocks)

Ensure that the enclosure has a hotspot on one end of and a cool spot on the other. You should provide a basking spot temperature of around 100 degrees Fahrenheit or more and an ambient temperature of 80 degrees Fahrenheit. The heat under or over the basking spot is suitable as long as your snake has a cooler side to retreat on after basking. Slightly cooler temperatures are acceptable at night or whenever your Burmese python is breeding.

Some reminders:

- All artificial heating sources should be kept outside of the cage so as to protect the snake from being burned.

- Always manually check the cage with a regular thermometer to confirm the readings of your thermostat as it can sometimes be inaccurate.

In terms of humidity levels, your Burmese python's enclosure should be kept at 60 percent humidity. If the humidity is extremely low, a daily misting will provide a higher humidity. Humidity should be maintained so as not to dry up the cage (and your pet) once you add heating equipment or once the temperature rises. It should have proper moisture because it also aids in proper shedding.

Lighting Guidelines

- Snakes in general need at least 12 hours of light followed by 12 hours of darkness. A simple timer can help you regulate the lighting cycle.

- Never use regular light bulbs that you can buy from your hardware store as there are specialized lights for reptiles that you can purchase from pet stores.

What's the purpose of lighting?

Proper lighting provides your pet with UV light because it will supply your pet with the proper amount of UVA and UVB rays that your Burmese python will use in regulating their metabolism, synthesizing vitamins and minerals as well as absorbing calcium to help keep their bones strong. These types of lightning sources are intended to mimic natural sunlight as much as possible.

Chapter Five: Nutrition and Feeding

The diet of your Burmese python in the wild may not be entirely the same during captivity. The amount of food they'll eat and how often they will eat is entirely up to you as the owner, so it's either you set up a new feeding schedule or you follow the breeder's recommended feeding guidelines to maintain how they were raised. Feeding a snake is very exciting for newbies or first – time Burmese python keepers as you will see how these creatures have different ways of consuming their prey. However, as exciting as it may be, it's always recommended that you take precautionary measures whenever you're feeding these animals especially once they grow bigger. Always prioritize safety – this goes the same for expert owners.

Burmese Pythons Food in the Wild

Snakes in general including the Burmese Python of course are carnivores. They primarily feed on mammals and birds both large and small. Adult Burmese snakes also loves hunting for pigs and deer in the wild while hatchlings and juveniles mostly consume rats, lizards, small birds, frogs, fish, and other reptiles commonly found in the wild.

The main concern for Burmese python is that since most of them are being released in the wild particularly in Everglades, Florida, they are now destroying the wildlife because they are constantly preying on birds and mammals and even alligators.

Burmese Python Feeding Facts:

- Burmese pythons like most snakes have very poor vision and the only way they can hunt for food is through flickering their tongues in order to stalk their potential prey. A snake's tongue has built – in chemical receptors and also heat sensors allowing them to know their surroundings, find prey and also fight off potential threats.

- The way they ambush their prey is through using a sit and wait method. This is very common among python species since most of them are non – venomous compared to vipers, which is why their only way to attack a prey is to be in a position for a kill. What they do is they submerged under the water or blend in the forest ground until they can grab their unsuspecting prey and kill it by constricting it, until the animal can't breathe anymore before chomping them up with their sharp teeth.

- Most Burmese pythons in the wild feed only a few times in a year because they usually take lots of time to digest their food.

Hatchling Feeding

Baby Burmese snakes can already eat an adult mouse during their first feedings. This is quite surprising for many first time python keepers because usually baby snakes starts eating only pinky mouse or small – sized prey, obviously not for Burmese pythons.

Here are some reminders for easy feeding:

- The food items should smell like food to attract their sensory receptors.

- The food should be fed in a way where it's a potential meal. Don't just left it lying on the ground, serve it as if it was a prey.

- The food should be at least warm enough than the surroundings. This is because pythons love to eat warm – blooded animals and this is what attracts them to eat the food. In this way, you'll be able to train the newborn babies to elicit a feeding response that will make them easy to feed and not become picky eaters as they grow old.

- After feeding a baby Burmese python in the first few days or weeks, you'll eventually notice that he will slowly get used to eating pre – killed frozen items.

Juvenile and Adult Burmese Python Feeding

- Of course as your pet grows, it will eventually require much larger prey items but lesser eating time.

- You need to feed them possibly more than one prey item; it depends on your snake's appetite though, so if you see that your pet is constantly eating, you might want to reduce the size of the prey.

- Feeding them once or twice a week is already ideal for a growing snake.

- Once it reaches 4 feet long, you can try feeding it with a medium sized rat. When it reaches 6 feet or longer, you can already feed it with an adult sized rat, young rabbit, or adult sized chicken.

Chapter Six: Maintenance for Burmese Pythons

If you want your snake to live a happy and long life, all you have to do is set up a great environment for them. Now that you have knowledge on what to feed them, when to feed them as well as properly set up the right cage for them, it's time you learn on how to maintain this kind of adequate environment. Maintaining cleanliness and hygiene for your pet Burmese python will definitely go a long way especially in terms of its health and overall well – being. They won't feel stressed, they won't be prone to diseases, and they will surely enjoy their time with your company. This chapter will provide you with tips about maintenance.

Bathing Your Burmese Python

Before cleaning your pet's terrarium or enclosure, it's ideal to bathe your pet first so that he'll be nice and clean once he transfer to his newly cleaned enclosure. You can of course, clean first the terrarium before bathing your pet it's entirely up to you. Some recommend placing your snake in a holding cage immediately after a bath as some snakes can defecate immediately after a bath, and you don't want him doing this too soon within the newly cleaned cage. Give your python sufficient time in the holding cage to do his business before moving him back to his home.

Benefits of Bathing Your Pet

An occasional bath for your Burmese Python can go a long way to having a happy and healthy snake. You don't need to scrub them or use any bathing materials like soaps or shampoo. Never use such items as it can be poisonous for your pet. Plain lukewarm water is fine.

- Bathing can help relieve constipation
- It can also kill mites
- Promotes proper shedding

Step – by – Step Bathing for Your Snake

Step #1: Use warm spring or filtered water. Don't use tap or chlorinated water as the chemicals in the water can actually irritate their skin. A good range between 100 and 105 degrees Fahrenheit is a good level for a snake bath. And because they are sensitive to temperature changes, you'll want to provide them with a reasonably warm bath.

Step #2: You can help your snake get into the bath, but more often than not, they will quickly bathe themselves. Just assist them but let them roam around on their own, they know what to do.

Step #3: Keep an eye on your pet during bathing. Never left your Burmese python unsupervised. You don't want your pet getting away from you during bathing time; you might want to place a sufficiently roomy bowl of the warm bath water in an enclosure.

Step #4: Just let your Burmese Python swim freely around in the water. If it shows signs of agitation, take it out immediately. Otherwise, let it soak around for 10 to 15 minutes.

Step #5: After bathing time, pick it up, and gently use a towel to dry it off. It's now to time return to his now clean, sterilized, disinfected, and thoroughly dried habitat or temporary cage (whichever you decided to clean first).

Tips on Spot - Cleaning

In order to spot – clean your pet's enclosure, follow the guidelines below:

Pre – Cleaning Tips

Tip #1: You will need to first temporarily relocate your Burmese python to a different terrarium. You can even relocate them to a plastic box that will be suitable for their size as long as this holding cell is secure and clean and properly ventilated. A medium-sized tank with a lid and air holes will do or another smaller.

Tip #2: Check for components. Just like when cleaning your house, you need to do a quick "scan" first to have an orderly manner of what materials you'll need to clean or even replace such as the bedding of the cage etc.

Tip #3: Buy cleaning materials that are chemical – free or snake proof. Make sure when you buy things like paper towels, disinfectants, water sprayer, trash bag, spray bottle, brushes, buckets, sponges, gloves, and other materials they are safe for your snake and will not leave any chemical residue that could potentially harm your pet after cleaning.

Tip #4: Unplug all the electrical devices on the cage. This includes your basking lamp and under tank heater or other heat source. Remove your gauges or thermometers as well.

Step – by – Step Cleaning

Step #1: Remove all the cage furniture items and decorations. Water bowls, hides, branches, rocks, plants and substrate. You can place them in the bathtub or sink where you'll wash them. You can also replace old substrate with new bedding. If your bedding of choice is shavings or coconut fiber and the likes, you can easily dump it or use a vacuum.

Step #2: Clean the empty cage. Use a spray bottle with water and paper towels to clear the dust, feces, and other dirt. Afterwards, use an antibacterial disinfectant.

Step #3: Leave the cage open and let it dry. You can also wipe the glasses clean with a soft cloth or rug so it can finish drying completely while you clean the other items.

Step #4: Clean the cage items with antibacterial soap and hot water. You may soak some items overnight in a diluted bleach solution if you have difficulty getting the dirt out. Do not scrub plastic bowls with fingernails or scouring pads. It will leave scratches on the bowl and it will make it harder to clean in the future. Instead, use the smooth part of your finger to rub the bowl clean, or soak it overnight.

Step #5: Make sure to clean the water bowl. Rinse it with hot water thoroughly with antibacterial soap and hot water.

You can also use water cleaner that you can purchase from pet stores to make sure that your water is safe for your snake.

Post – Cleaning Tips

Tip #1: Add new bedding and replace the furniture (optional). You can also just return the materials you cleaned in the cage and don't forget to fill up the bowl with fresh water.

Tip #2: Relocate your snake to its newly cleaned terrarium and plug in the electrical devices. Make sure all the locks and latches are secure, and clean up your separate tank or the temporary cage as well.

Tip #3: Clean the temporary tank. You'll also need to clean the temporary tank so that you can make sure that it is clean for the next use.

Chapter Seven: Handling Your Burmese Python

Some snake species are easy to deal with when it comes to feeding them. However, there are still some species out there that might be a bit aggressive so it's important that you also learn on how to socialize and tame these pets if ever they get defensive. This chapter will teach you some basic handling skills, how to feed them especially on their first few days, and some frequently ask questions about taming aggressive behavior of snakes just in case your pet will have trouble adjusting with its new environment.

Handling Your New Pet Burmese Python

Once you brought your new pet home, it's wise to let the snake adjust to its new environment and as much as possible don't bother them for at least for a few days. You'll notice it consistently flicking its tongue because it's trying to make sense of its new environment so just let them be and as days go on gradually introduce yourself to them. Here are some tips on how you can start a good relationship with your new pet:

Tip #1: Allow your Burmese Python to adjust to you. It is normal for them to hide or defend themselves, but they cannot really harm you (since they are non – venomous) unless of course you sort of taunt them.

Tip #2: Let it sit outside its terrarium for a few days. What you need to do as soon as your snake arrives especially in the first few days is to just let them roam around the house (supervised) for about an hour each day and allow your pet to get used to your smell.

Tip#3: Try to resist constantly touching your new snake during these first few weeks. Give your new pet a few weeks to settle into its home and get used to a regular feeding routine. Remember, snakes are also living beings that need to settle and get used to new spaces.

Tip #4: Try not to stress it out with unnecessary handling during the "adjusting period." At the end of this initial week, you can now begin to move things around inside your snake's terrarium. However, it is still not allowed to attempt to touch your pet python at this point. Continuously do this for another week so that your snake can get used to the idea that you have no intention to harm him. Being around it without attempting to touch it will let your Burmese python know that you are not a danger or threat.

Tip #5: Start to gently touch it after a week or so inside the terrarium. Once you think that your snake know that you are not a threat, you can start to touch it while inside its cage by placing your hand in its cage and gently start touching it, moving it around inside the cage, and lifting your snake's tail. Continue doing this manner to your snake for three to four days.

Tip #6: Start handling it for short periods of time outside of the cage. Once you see that your pet is comfortable with its new surroundings, you can start approaching your snake. However, do not handle it for the first two to three days after a meal.

Tip #7: Approach your snake from the side. Avoid handling it as if you're a predator as what predators do is that they would approach it from the top, so do it from the side. Then slowly but confidently lift it. Hesitation will scare your snake and will cause it to hide or bite. When your Burmese python realizes you are not going to eat it, it will calm down and tame quickly. Eventually, it will become used to handling.

Guidelines for Proper Handling of Your Snake

It's very important that you pay attention to the snake's responses so that you'll know how to approach it. Your pet's reaction will vary based on the stress they may feel or how you interact with them.

- **Remember to always to keep calm and to make your actions slow and deliberate.** Don't rush and don't hesitate especially when picking them up. They can smell fear from a mile away! If this happens, they'll be harder to handle and may also think of you as a foe not a friend.

- **Touch them regularly or at certain times so that they'll get used to you and your smell.** They'll eventually get more used to touching and handling as long as you do it right. Burmese pythons are relatively tolerant of human touch; just approach them the right way.

- **Never pick your Burmese python up by the head**. Almost all snakes tend to thoroughly dislike being petted on their head, as it makes them feel like you are a predator exerting dominance. This will stress them out and may cause them to attack you as instincts will kick in.

- **Never pick up your snake by the tail too!** Doing so may cause it to thrash around in your grip and may end up injuring itself.

- **Learn to support your snake's body during handling.** Lift your pet snake from the mid-body area so that it will relax better in your grip.

- **Be extra careful in handling juvenile Burmese pythons**. Be prepared for the possibilities that it may crawl away from you or they can be quite wiggly when handled.

- **Be sensitive and observe how they react to your touch.** Pay attention to how your Burmese python responds to your movements.

Some Behavioral Facts about Burmese Pythons

Knowing the behavior of your pet Burmese will surely aid you whenever you're handling them, feeding them or giving them a bath. It will also help you distinguish if they're feeling stressed out, agitated or if they are feeling sick. Of course, every Burmese python have their own set of unique and individual characteristics, and you as the keeper will eventually become familiar with it after months of keeping them.

Here are the general behavioral traits of Burmese pythons:

- Burmese pythons are terrestrial snake species, which means that they will spend most of their time low on the ground. They are also nocturnal, doing most of their activities at night, and they are usually most active in the morning.

- As what established many times in this book, Burmese pythons are constrictors – using their sharp, backward-curving teeth, they will grasp their prey to restrain it, and then wrap it around with coils.

- Sometimes juvenile Burmese pythons get extremely agitated and stressed if their enclosure is too big for them. They sometimes stop eating because they are daunted by the large space. Small enclosures make them feel secure so make sure that the cage or enclosure is appropriate for their size.

- These are ambush predators. They avoid detection, seek cover, and wait for their prey. Their hiding skills involve camouflage which works very well in their natural habitat in forests and grasslands.

- Most pythons have infrared-sensitive receptors in their snout, which allows them to sense the radiated heat of warm-blooded prey. They use their forked tongues to both "smell" and taste their potential food or a potential threat. They can also perceive movement through their undersides, which are sensitive to vibrations in the ground. It only goes to say that you can't sneak up on these guys!

- Prior to shedding, the snake stops eating and retreats or hides in a safe place. The inner surface of the skin sort of become liquefied in order to separate the old skin from the new skin. When the snake is ready – typically after a few days – the eyes clear again and the snake crawls out of its old skin. The new skin is typically larger and brighter than the old one. Their skin becomes dull and dry looking, and their eyes turn cloudy or blue-colored.

- While adult snakes may shed its skin only once or twice a year, younger or juvenile and growing snakes can shed up to 3 to 4 times a year.

Chapter Eight: Breeding Your Burmese Python

Keeping a Burmese python is already a huge undertaking as it will definitely take most of your time and effort as well as affect your household budget. Keeping more than one Burmese python means that you are really passionate about taking care of these pets and you somehow have proven to yourself that you are indeed a responsible keeper. However, breeding Burmese pythons is a different ball game. You won't only take care of one baby python, you might be taking care of a bunch of them – by bunch I mean more or less 12 t0 30 eggs plus of course the mother, and oh some even lay 100 eggs in a clutch, that's just in 1 year!

There's a huge possibility that the mother Burmese python can continuously lay more eggs year after year especially if it is housed with a male species. If you don't have the knowledge and expertise as well as the financial capacity of taking care the first 100 eggs, then maybe just keeping one or two is best. But if this is an endeavor you sincerely and passionately wanted to take, then this chapter is for you. You'll learn about the basics of breeding Burmese pythons in this chapter.

FAQs about Breeding a Burmese Python

Is it hard to breed snakes?

Breeding snakes is not as hard as it may seem but before anything else you have to make sure that if you are going to breed a snake, you have to get in their heads and think about breeding in a way that a snake will think about breeding in the environment or in the wild.

Why is it important that I set up the right breeding conditions?

You have to learn about the conditions needed and the triggers to make your Burmese python breed. In the wild, if the conditions are not good, and the mother snake will just decide not to breed or lay eggs because they know that their babies will not survive or even thrive in such an environment. With that being said, you need to keep in mind that for you to successfully breed your Burmese python, you should know how to set up the right breeding conditions. If the environment, temperature, and food is good or abundant, the mother snake will feel comfortable giving birth because she knows her babies can thrive in this kind of environment.

What is the right temperature for breeding?

As previously mentioned, the ambient temperature for Burmese python should be around 80 degrees Fahrenheit, and the cool side of the enclosure should have less than 80 degrees. Burmese pythons usually breed around the months of November to February and their eggs are laid around March to April so during breeding time you can already set a warmer temperature.

Breeding Tips

Tip #1: Cool them down. In order to prep your Burmese python, what you can do is cool them down at around five degrees lower than the ambient temperature degrees for six to eight hours every day from November to February. Once you have these conditions ready you can now move to checking out the follicle growth of your pet.

Tip #2: Check to see if there are follicles. You can find the follicles of your female python just near the gallbladder. However, you may need to use an ultrasound or maybe take a trip to the vet and find out if there's any growth in its follicles.

Tip #3: Measure the follicles. Usually, if your snake's follicles measure about ten to twelve millimeters that could be a good starting point for breeding, although it may be different for other snake species but it is usually the average size that you need. These follicles are a sign that your female is ready for breeding.

Tip #4: Measure the follicles without going to the vet. If you don't have an ultrasound or going to the vet may seem costly, what you can do to measure the snake's follicle is through feeling the bumps on your snake's body. Its follicles are located about two – thirds down the body almost before its tail. What you can do is get your snake out of the cage, and then have her go back inside the enclosure while holding her and letting their body run through your fingers. You can also tickle their tail a little bit to get her going inside. However, do not rub or slide your fingers down its body because you're not going to feel anything. What you should do is to just let her crawl through your hand, while pinching your fingers in its body a little bit so you can feel the follicle bumps.

Tip #5: Schedule the copulation. Once you get the conditions right and hit the right number of follicle measurement, that means you can start breeding them or copulating them with a male Burmese python at least every 3 to 4 weeks but be sure to let them rest after a few weeks of copulation.

Tip #6: Continue the copulation process. You can start copulating it again with a male once its follicles hits twenty millimeters, until the follicle hits about thirty millimeters. When it does, you can check it again using an ultrasound to see if she is beginning to ovulate.

Tip #7: Measure the follicles after initial copulation. If the follicles measure around thirty five to forty millimeters that means that your female snake will start its ovulation process within two weeks.

Tip #8: Adjust their feeding amount/ frequency. Within a couple days of your female snake breeding, you want to give them more food. Feed her as much as she will eat or at least more than her normal food range, they'll also eventually stop eating on their own.

Breeding Facts for Burmese Pythons

- The mating or breeding season for Burmese pythons happens from November to February. Egg laying occurs from March to April.

- The incubation period will take about 60 to 80 days.

- During the incubation period, the Burmese python will wrap itself around her eggs so as to generate heat and maintain the temperature of its eggs. The muscle strain during breeding season may cause your pet snake to lose half of its weight.

- The average clutch size of a Burmese python is around 12 to 30 eggs or more (it varies depending on the individual species). Some Burmese pythons even lay 100 eggs in 1 year.

- At hatching, a neonate Burmese python measures approximately 18 to 29 inches in length and weighs in at an average of 4 ounces.

- These baby Burmese pythons will reach sexual maturity after 2 to 3 years.

Breeding Materials and Nesting Guidelines

Below are some tips on the kinds of things you need to provide for your female pet Burmese during breeding season so that you can properly accommodate the newly born eggs.

Suggested Nesting Materials:

- **Nesting Box:** Either made out of wood or plastic, with a lid and an entrance hole large enough to accommodate the passage of two coils of her body at the same time. Some can use an improvised box, lidded plastic buckets, ice cream containers or overturned flower pots.

- **Nesting Box Size Requirement:** 8 x 8 inches wide and length; 12 inches in height.

- **Bedding:** Substrate or bedding should be provided at the bottom of the nesting box to prevent the eggs from sticking to the box itself. Some make good use of dry sphagnum moss, newspaper or coconut fiber.

Tips before Egg Laying

- **Be careful where you place the box in the cage.** Make sure that it is not directly connected or near a light and heat source or you risk overheating the eggs.

- **Provide thick bedding underneath the nesting box.** Some snakes lay the eggs directly while they are on the perch and not on the nesting box you provided, so you need to provide thick bedding at the bottom of the cage to help cushion the eggs as they fall.

- **Reduce water in the water bowl.** Some snakes choose to lay their eggs in the water bowl. In order to prevent the eggs from drowning, what you need to do is reduce the water content in the bowl to at least a centimeter or so when the time is nearing for the female to lay her eggs.

Tips during Incubation

- **Be observant of the mother snake's health.** Females typically refuse eating from the period of ovulation until hatching, and coupled with the physical demand of having produced and laid the eggs, the female's physical condition is at risk of deteriorating quite rapidly. A significant amount of weight loss is to be expected making her recovery much harder.

- **Examine the eggs.** A single bad egg can cause the entire clutch to deteriorate, since the eggs typically adhere to each other. Some form of monitoring or examination of the eggs is important.

- **Slowly and gently remove the eggs from their mom's constraint for proper incubation.** You need to remove the female from the eggs around which she would have coiled. Simply lift her coils until she is removed from the eggs. Be cautious though especially if you are dealing with a more aggressive female and that's of course understandable because she is just protecting her young.

- **Separate the eggs.** The eggs will often be stuck together in a clump. Separate them carefully and place them in individual trays to prevent bad or rotting eggs from contaminating the rest. Be careful as you do this so you do not tear the eggs.

- **Open the container to promote air exchange.** Do this at least once a week at first, then at least daily within the final week near hatching. Make sure that no condensation forms on the lid of the container which can cause moisture to drip down into the eggs as this can cause the eggs to spoil. As much as possible, the eggs should not come into contact with or be exposed to wet or moist surfaces.

- **The incubation container's temperature should be maintained.** The temperature should be around 80 to 84 degrees. Humidity levels should also be maintained at above 90 to 100 percent throughout the incubation period. The incubation period lasts for around 60 to 80 days before you can expect it to hatch.

Hatching Tips

- **Replace the water and provide a perch.** Make sure to replace the water at the bottom of the container with damp paper towels to prevent the drowning of any hatchlings that may emerge. You may also provide a perch or two to provide them a place to rest after they have emerged from the egg.

- **Never try to pull the hatchling out.** They have sharp teeth so it's fine not to help them out of the egg because they could still be absorbing some of the yolk from inside the egg.

- **Make sure that they have individual tubs.** Each of them should be set up in an individual plastic tubs where they should be kept well-hydrated until they shed. Provide them with a simple perch, a water bowl, and a heat source.

Chapter Nine: Common Diseases of Burmese Pythons

This chapter will focus on the diseases that are common among Burmese pythons. Make sure to read this chapter so that you'll have an idea on what to do in case your pet python catches an illness. You'll be given an overview, symptoms, treatments (if any), and prevention tips so that you can ensure that your snake will not only live a healthy life but also maximize its lifespan and of course not be a financial burden on your part.

Common Health Problems

In this section, you will be provided with some of the most common health problems affecting Burmese pythons. Prevention is always better than cure!

IBD (Inclusion Body Disease)

Overview:

- Inclusion body disease (IBD) is a very serious viral disease.
- It may attack your Burmese python's respiratory or digestive track, but generally it goes for the snake's nervous system.

Symptoms, Treatment, Prevention:

- If your Burmese Python has IBD it will not be able to lie on its back and may even be paralyzed.
- Snakes diagnosed with IBD are euthanized because there is no existing cure as of yet.

Stomatitis or Mouth Rot

Overview:

- It is an infection of the snake's oral cavity.
- There is usually an excessive amount of mucus, sometimes there's also blood found in the mouth and at the inside edge of the lips.

Symptoms, Treatment, Prevention:

- A presence of pus or a white substance in the mouth.
- Loss of teeth
- Swollen mouth
- Open-mouth breathing
- Loss of appetite

- To cure stomatitis, injectable antibiotics would have to be administered to your pet. Its mouth would also have to be thoroughly cleaned with antibiotic solutions.

- To prevent it from worsening, immediately consult the veterinarian when you think your pet has acquired stomatitis because it can be fatal if left untreated.

Parasitism

Overview:

- Internal parasites include various worms, while external parasites include tick and mites.
- There is often no visible signs that your snake is infected with parasites, and its usually veterinary check-ups that will reveal the illness which is why routine checkup is quite important.

Symptoms, Treatment, Prevention:

- Problem in breathing
- Diarrhea
- Regurgitation or vomiting
- Scale irritation and skin infection
- Weight loss
- Swelling of internal organs

- There are available medications to deworm the snake, which can be either ingested or injected.

- Proper husbandry, hygiene and clean thawed food may prevent parasitism

Rectal Prolapse

Overview:

- Rectal prolapse takes place when the bowel protrudes outside of the cloaca during defecation, whereby the snake subsequently is unable to retract it.
- Some vets suggest that inappropriate diet could be the cause, though other contributing factors may also be the reason. Such factors include obesity, stress, and lack of muscle tone.

Symptoms, Treatment, Prevention:

- Lethargy
- Loss of Appetite
- Dehydration
- Painful defecation

- Make sure to keep your snake well hydrated through their food, available fresh water, and humid conditions within the tank.

- Have a good, sizeable enclosure for your pet, with various perches to choose from because this encourages exercise and movement that can prevent this condition from developing in the first place.

- Let your pet roam around the house or your backyard to introduce movement and exercise but make sure they are supervised or they only roam in places that are also secure.

- Bring your snake to a vet for proper treatment of rectal prolapse.

- A form of adhesive material will be administered. This material can be easily pulled off. It is used around the cloaca to prevent a reoccurrence of the prolapsed. This consists of moistening the swollen tissue and reinserting it back into place. This should be followed by withholding food for about two weeks, followed by controlled feeding of small prey until bowel movement normalizes.

Tail – Hanging

Overview:

- Tail hanging occurs when fecal matter accumulates, sometimes becoming very dry, making your snake no longer comfortable to wrap around its perch, and is often simply left to hang suspended from its perch.

Symptoms, Treatment, Prevention:

- This is similar to constipation among snakes, and is often related to or eventually causes rectal prolapse. Treatment will almost be the same; a form of adhesive material will be administered unless of course the vet says otherwise.

- Some form of exercise would help build your snake's muscle tone and also promote healthier digestive processes.

- This can possibly be prevented by integrating regular schedules and lifestyle routines that promote movement, exercise, and hydration in your pet snake.

Lung Infections

Overview:

Respiratory disease is typically caused by bacteria, though some other causes are parasites, viruses, and fungi.

Symptoms, Treatment, Prevention:

- Excess mucus in their oral cavities
- Excessive nasal discharges
- Loss of appetite
- Wheezing
- Gurgling sounds
- Open-mouth breathing

- The veterinarian may take X-rays, blood tests, and cultures to determine the root cause of the disease.

- Treatment usually includes antibiotics, which may be administered orally, through injection or by nose drops.

- Snakes suffering from respiratory disease require intensive care, which may include fluid therapy and force feeding.

Dermatitis

Overview:

- Dermatitis in Burmese pythons is usually caused by an unclean habitat or damp surroundings, and it is typically characterized by blisters and rapid shedding.

- The initial vesicles are filled with fluid and do not have any bacteria but if the conditions are not corrected, any bacterial organisms found in or on the snake or its environment may infect the vesicles.

- If left untreated the bacteria can spread through the bloodstream and could also cause septicemia. In severe cases, death can occur in a matter of days.

Symptoms, Treatment, Prevention:

- If you think your pet Burmese has this disease, then you should immediately place it in a dry environment and fix the humidity in its enclosure. Clean the habitat as well.

- Go to the veterinarian before it gets worse.

- To determine which antibiotic treatment is best for your pet, the veterinarian will have to perform diagnosis which may include a biopsy or cytology and a bacterial culture and sensitivity.

Toxemia

Overview:

- Toxemia is a disease where microbes invade the bloodstream and other organs.

- When a snake has toxemia, it becomes critically ill and may even be near-death.

Symptoms, Treatment, Prevention:

- Lethargy
- Lack of appetite
- Red discoloration on the snake's belly
- Open-mouth breathing

- Antibiotics and fluid therapy must be administered, and sometimes force-feeding is even necessary.
- Bring it immediately to the veterinarian.

Chapter Ten: Care Sheet and Summary

Learning new things about your pet Burmese Python doesn't stop here. You should always make an effort in knowing more about this breed so that you can be a better care taker. Keep in mind that these pets already has a vulnerable status under some wildlife organizations, which is why it's essential that you take care of these species properly by following right husbandry practices.

It's also highly recommended that you also talk with other Burmese python breeders or other snake experts so that you can stay updated especially in terms of your snake's health and licensing rules. Aside from gaining new insights from fellow enthusiasts, you can also make new friends and also be part of a community.

Biological Information

Taxonomy: Python molurus bivittatus. They belong in Kingdom Animalia, Phylum Chordata, Class Reptilia, Order Squamata, Family Boidae, Genus Python molorus, and Species bivittatus.

Country of Origin: Asia and Southeast Asia including Pakistan, Eastern India, Nepal, Srilanka, Indonesia, China (southern area), Burma, Celeb Islands, Borneo, Sumatra, Bhutan, Bangladesh, Laos, Vietnam, Myanmar, Cambodia, Thailand, Bali, Sumbawa and Java except the Philippines. They are mostly found in dry jungles, mountains, grasslands, grassy marshes and sometimes in rivers, rocky foothills, valleys, and swamps.

Size: The average adult size is 15 to 20 feet or 5 to 6 meters, hatchlings and juveniles usually reach up to 24 inches or 60 centimeters or more.

Weight: The average weight for an adult Burmese python is 200 pounds or 90 kilograms!

Color: Their skin color is dark brown coupled with spots of beige resembling a puzzle piece or skin patterns found in a giraffe (which is why people in the leather manufacturing industry are coming after them). They can also be distinguished by the 2 lines that run on their heads just across both of their eyes.

Body Type and Appearance: Their skin color is dark brown coupled with spots of beige; they can also be distinguished by the 2 lines that run on their heads just across both of their eyes. It has skin patterns that can camouflage into any grassy or forestry environment; has smooth silky skin and scales and the lower jaws of Burmese pythons can open up independently enabling them to fully swallow their prey.

Food in the Wild: These snakes prey on different mammals, reptiles (big or small) as well as birds. They are also notorious for eating huge mammals like deer and pigs.

Breeding Distinction: Burmese python shows rather a much better parental care compared to other reptile species because they incubate the eggs they lay using their own muscle to generate heat.

Temperament: docile and non – venomous but can be aggressive when threatened.

Health Conditions: generally healthy but predisposed to common illnesses such as IBD (Inclusion Body Disease), Stomatitis or Mouth Rot, Parasitism, Rectal Prolapse, Tail – Hanging, Lung Infections, Dermatitis, and Toxemia

Lifespan: Their lifespan is quite long especially if they live in the wild; on average they live for about 20 - 25 years. In fact, the longest living Burmese python ever recorded lasted for 28 years and nearly 3 months.

Wildlife Conservation Status: Burmese Pythons are listed in the Appendix II of the CITES and labeled as Vulnerable or (have risk of being endangered) by other organizations including the IUCN.

What Makes Burmese Pythons Ideal as Pets

- Questions to Consider Before Acquring a Burmese Python:
- Do you have enough knowledge and experience in handling or keeping snakes?
- Can you provide an adequate living condition for them?
- Can you take the time to learn how to take care of them from hatchlings until they reach adulthood?
- Can you afford to buy everything they need including its diet, cage or enclosures, permits, habitat maintenance materials, veterinary expenses in cases of medical emergencies etc?
- Can you handle the breeding process and breeding maintenance of your snake if ever you decided to breed them?
- Can you handle bites from time to time? All snake keepers even if their pet is docile still get bitten every now and then – it's part of the job, do you think you can handle that?

- Are your friends and family okay with keeping a snake as pets?

Temperament: Burmese pythons are docile, non – venomous and can adapt with human contact especially if they are being handled at an early age. Their non – venomous and also non – aggressive nature makes them ideal as family pets even if you have kids.

Other pets: In terms of housing them with other household pets, your dog or cat is safe as long as they don't come anywhere near the cage or enclosure of your Burmese python since these animals prey on mammals, it's better to keep your other pets away from the snake to avoid any casualties.

Major Pro: Burmese Pythons are aesthetically appealing creatures; these snakes have a docile and people – friendly temperament. Burmese Pythons will surely keep any expert snake keeper on their feet. Maintenance can be quite challenging but also fun.

Major Con: Burmese Pythons does get very long and heavy. If you aren't prepared to handle a 200 pound snake, maybe it's not for you. These pets are quite sensitive to temperature and humidity changes, so you would have to be extra careful to make sure that they are comfortable.

Legal Requirements and Snake Licensing:

- The Burmese Python is included in Appendix II of the Convention on International Trade in Endangered Species of Wild Fauna and Flora or CITES wherein the international trade involving it is monitored and regulated.
- There is no federal law governing private possession or ownership of exotic animals in the United States.
- You need to pay attention not on a national level but on a local level to see what is permitted and what is not.
- Make sure to check the rules about keeping pet snakes based on where you are to avoid penalties or confiscation of your pet. You might not even be able to find a veterinarian willing to give your Burmese Python medical care if you are found to be keeping it without the correct permits.
- Permits may also be necessary for importing, exporting, or traveling with an exotic or a naturally dangerous animal.

Basic Keeping Materials Checklist

- Purchase price: $200 - $500
- Glass Enclosure with a screen top or lid: approx. $100 (depending on size)

- Bedding or Substrate: $10
- Water Dish: $10 - $15 (depending on size/quality)
- Under Tank Heater: $25 or more
- Basking Lamp: $30 or more
- Heat and Water Temperature Regulator/ Gauges: $5 or more (often comes with the under tank heater/basking lamp)
- Hiding Place: $5 - $10
- Feeding tank: $30 - $50 or more
- Food: $10 - $15 (depending on brand and amount)
- Vet bills: $75 or more
- License/Permit: depends on the state/country you live in.

Purchasing and Selecting a Healthy Breed

Where to Purchase:

- Large or Major Pet Stores
- Reptile Conventions or Snake Expos
- Private Breeders
- Online Sellers/Pet Stores

Advantages of Buying from a Private Breeder: You'll know the following information:

- Bloodline/ Lineage / Family History (for possible disease history/ genetics)
- Husbandry Needs (Temperature, Lighting, Environmental Condition)
- Nutrition (Diet, Food Amount, Frequency)
- Medical History (Vaccines (if any))
- Personality/ Temperament of the Species

Home-based Breeders vs. Business Breeders

- Breeders range from large-scale operations to small-scale, private setups.
- Breeders with large budgets or those who breed for business have legit websites filled with snake facts and official sources, while some home-based breeders have blogs that detail personal accounts of handling snakes and other reptiles.
- Some breeders choose to go to more formal and traditional route by attending reptile expos and showing off their breeds.
- Most home – based business and medium – sized breeders just do their own promotion or even supply pet stores instead of putting up their own store.

Breeder Checklist

Tip #1: Look for snake breeders with good reputation.

Tip #2: Know what you want.

Tip #3: Look for breeders who are also finding "responsible keepers"

Tip #4: Better to Buy from Breeders near You

Tip #5: See Where the Action Happens

Signs of a Healthy Burmese Python

- Has a well-rounded body
- Clean and clear eyes and vent
- There should be no signs of respiratory problems, such as wheezing when held, mouth opening a lot, nasal discharge, and mucus around or large bubbles in the mouth.
- They should also be free of parasites such as ticks and mites.
- In terms of behavior, the Burmese python must be somewhat curious and open to your touch, gripping you when being handled.
- In terms of feeding practices, try to see how they respond to feeding from their breeder so that you'll

know if they are picky eaters or would have no problem whatsoever.

Habitat Requirements for Burmese Pythons:

How to Set Up Habitat for Your Snake:

- A young Burmese python's ideal cage size is a 10 – gallon tank or terrarium.
- Burmese pythons grow heavier over time, the floor space that they would need should be 4 x 8 (feet).
- The ground space should be 4 to 6 times larger or wider than your pet if he/she is in a coiled up position.
- Make sure that you also provide a door that can be both easily access and can also be tightly secured.
- You will also need a substrate because it will serve as the substitute for soil or ground just like how it is in their natural habitat in the wild. It will also serve as humidifiers inside the cage in order to control the temperature.

Regulating Temperature

- Temperatures in their natural habitat are around 70 – 80 degrees Fahrenheit so to be able to replicate this in a cage means providing supplemental heating sources.
- In terms of humidity levels, your Burmese python's enclosure should be kept at 60 percent humidity.
- All artificial heating sources should be kept outside of the cage so as to protect the snake from being burned.
- Always manually check the cage with a regular thermometer to confirm the readings of your thermostat as it can sometimes be inaccurate.

Lighting Guidelines

- Snakes in general need at least 12 hours of light followed by 12 hours of darkness. A simple timer can help you regulate the lighting cycle.
- Never use regular light bulbs that you can buy from your hardware store as there are specialized lights for reptiles that you can purchase from pet stores.

Nutritional Requirements

Burmese Python Feeding Facts:

- Burmese pythons like most snakes have very poor vision and the only way they can hunt for food is through flickering their tongues in order to stalk their potential prey. A snake's tongue has built – in chemical receptors and also heat sensors allowing them to know their surroundings, find prey and also fight off potential threats.
- The way they ambush their prey is through using a sit and wait method. This is very common among python species since most of them are non – venomous compared to vipers, which is why their only way to attack a prey is to be in a position for a kill. What they do is they submerged under the water or blend in the forest ground until they can grab their unsuspecting prey and kill it by constricting it, until the animal can't breathe anymore before chomping them up with their sharp teeth.
- Most Burmese pythons in the wild feed only a few times in a year because they usually take lots of time to digest their food.

Feeding Tips:

- The food items should smell like food to attract their sensory receptors.
- The food should be fed in a way where it's a potential meal. Don't just left it lying on the ground, serve it as if it was a prey.
- The food should be at least warm enough than the surroundings. This is because pythons love to eat warm – blooded animals and this is what attracts them to eat the food. In this way, you'll be able to train the newborn babies to elicit a feeding response that will make them easy to feed and not become picky eaters as they grow old.
- After feeding a baby Burmese python in the first few days or weeks, you'll eventually notice that he will slowly get used to eating pre – killed frozen items.

Maintenance for Burmese Python

Bathing Your Burmese Python

Step #1: Use warm spring or filtered water.

Step #2: You can help your snake get into the bath, but more often than not, they will quickly bathe themselves

Step #3: Keep an eye on your pet during bathing. Never left your Burmese python unsupervised.

Step #4: Just let your Burmese Python swim freely around in the water.

Step #5: After bathing time, pick it up, and gently use a towel to dry it off.

Tips on Spot - Cleaning

Pre – Cleaning Tips

Tip #1: You will need to first temporarily relocate your Burmese python to a different terrarium.

Tip #2: Check for components.

Tip #3: Buy cleaning materials that are chemical – free or snake proof.

Tip #4: Unplug all the electrical devices on the cage.

Post – Cleaning Tips

Tip #1: Add new bedding and replace the furniture (optional).

Tip #2: Relocate your snake to its newly cleaned terrarium and plug in the electrical devices.

Tip #3: Clean the temporary tank.

Step – by – Step Cleaning

Step #1: Remove all the cage furniture items and decorations.

Step #2: Clean the empty cage.

Step #3: Leave the cage open and let it dry.

Step #4: Clean the cage items with antibacterial soap and hot water.

Step #5: Make sure to clean the water bowl.

Handling Your Burmese Pythons

Tip #1: Allow your Burmese Python to adjust to you.

Tip #2: Let it sit outside its terrarium for a few days.

Tip#3: Try to resist constantly touching your new snake during these first few weeks.

Tip #4: Try not to stress it out with unnecessary handling during the "adjusting period."

Tip #5: Start to gently touch it after a week or so inside the terrarium.

Tip #6: Start handling it for short periods of time outside of the cage.

Tip #7: Approach your snake from the side.

Guidelines for Proper Handling of Your Snake

- Remember to always to keep calm and to make your actions slow and deliberate.
- Touch them regularly or at certain times so that they'll get used to you and your smell.
- Never pick your Burmese python up by the head.
- Never pick up your snake by the tail too!
- Learn to support your snake's body during handling.
- Be extra careful in handling juvenile Burmese pythons
- Be sensitive and observe how they react to your touch.

Behavioral Traits of Burmese pythons:

- Burmese pythons are terrestrial snake species, which means that they will spend most of their time low on the ground. They are also nocturnal, doing most of their activities at night, and they are usually most active in the morning.

- Most pythons have infrared-sensitive receptors in their snout, which allows them to sense the radiated heat of warm-blooded prey. They use their forked tongues to both "smell" and taste their potential food or a potential threat.

Breeding Your Burmese Pythons

Breeding Tips

Tip #1: Cool them down.

Tip #2: Check to see if there are follicles.

Tip #3: Measure the follicles.

Tip #4: Measure the follicles without going to the vet.

Tip #5: Schedule the copulation.

Tip #6: Continue the copulation process.

Tip #7: Measure the follicles after initial copulation.

Tip #8: Adjust their feeding amount/ frequency

Breeding Facts

- The mating or breeding season for Burmese pythons happens from November to February. Egg laying occurs from March to April.

- The incubation period will take about 60 to 80 days.
- During the incubation period, the Burmese python will wrap itself around her eggs so as to generate heat and maintain the temperature of its eggs. The muscle strain during breeding season may cause your pet snake to lose half of its weight.
- The average clutch size of a Burmese python is around 12 to 30 eggs or more (it varies depending on the individual species). Some Burmese pythons even lay 100 eggs in 1 year.

Breeding Materials

- **Nesting Box Size Requirement:** 8 x 8 inches wide and length; 12 inches in height.

- **Bedding:** Substrate or bedding should be provided at the bottom of the nesting box to prevent the eggs from sticking to the box itself.

Nesting Guidelines

- Be careful where you place the box in the cage.
- Provide thick bedding underneath the nesting box.
- Reduce water in the water bowl.

- Tips during Incubation
- Be observant of the mother snake's health.
- Examine the eggs.
- Slowly and gently remove the eggs from their mom's constraint for proper incubation.
- Separate the eggs.
- Open the container to promote air exchange.
- The incubation container's temperature should be maintained.

Hatching Tips

- Replace the water and provide a perch.
- Never try to pull the hatchling out.
- Make sure that they have individual tubs

Common Diseases

- IBD (Inclusion Body Disease)
- Parasitism
- Rectal Prolapse
- Tail – Hanging
- Lung Infections
- Dermatitis
- Toxemia

Glossary of Snake Terms

1.2.3. (Numbers with full stops) – The numbers are used to denote the number of a species, arranged according to sex, thus: male.female.unknown sex. In this case, one male, two females, and three of unknown sex.

Acclimation – Adjusting to a new environment or new conditions over a period of time.

Active range – The area of activity which can include hunting, seeking refuge, and finding a mate.

Ambient temperature – The overall temperature of the environment.

Amelanistic – Amel for short; without melanin, or without any black or brown coloration.

Anal Plate – A modified ventral scale that covers and protects the vent; sometimes a single plate, sometimes a divided plate.

Anerythristic – Anery for short; without any red coloration.

Aquatic – Lives in water.

Arboreal – Lives in trees.

Betadine – An antiseptic that can be used to clean wounds in reptiles.

Bilateral – Where stripes, spots or markings are present on both sides of an animal.

Biotic – The living components of an environment.

Brille – A transparent scale above the eyes of snakes that allows them to see but also serves to protect the eyes at the same time. Also called Spectacle, and Ocular Scale.

Brumation – The equivalent of mammalian hibernation among reptiles.

Cannibalistic – Where an animal feeds on others of its own kind.

Caudocephalic Waves – The ripple-like contractions that move from the rear to the front of a snake's body.

CB – Captive Bred, or bred in captivity.

CH – Captive Hatched.

Cloaca – also Vent; a half-moon shaped opening for digestive waste disposal and sexual organs.

Cloacal Gaping – Indication of sexual receptivity of the female.

Cloacal Gland – A gland at the base of the tail which emits foul smelling liquid as a defense mechanism; also called Anal Gland.

Clutch – A batch of eggs.

Constriction – The act of wrapping or coiling around a prey to subdue and kill it prior to eating.

Crepuscular – Active at twilight, usually from dusk to dawn.

Crypsis – Camouflage or concealing.

Diurnal – Active by day

Drop – To lay eggs or to bear live young.

Ectothermic – Cold-blooded. An animal that cannot regulate its own body temperature, but sources body heat from the surroundings.

Endemic – Indigenous to a specific region or area.

Estivation – Also Aestivation; a period of dormancy that usually occurs during the hot or dry seasons in order to escape the heat or to remain hydrated.

Faunarium (Faun) – A plastic enclosure with an air holed lid, usually used for small animals such as hatchling snakes, lizards, and insects.

FK – Fresh Killed; a term usually used when feeding a rodent that is recently killed, and therefore still warm, to a pet snake.

Flexarium – A reptile enclosure that is mostly made from mesh screening, for species that require plenty of ventilation.

Fossorial – A burrowing species.

Fuzzy – For rodent prey, one that has just reached the stage of development where fur is starting to grow.

F/T – Frozen/thawed; used to refer to food items that are frozen but thawed before feeding to your pet.

Gestation – The period of development of an embryo within a female.

Gravid – The equivalent of pregnant in reptiles.

Glottis – A tube-like structure that projects from the lower jaw of a snake to facilitate ingestion of large food items.

Gut-loading – Feeding insects within 24 hours to a prey before they are fed to your pet, so that they pass on the nutritional benefits.

Hatchling – A newly hatched, or baby, reptile.

Hemipenes – Dual sex organs; common among male snakes.

Hemipenis – A single protrusion of a paired sexual organ; one half is used during copulation.

Herps/Herpetiles – A collective name for reptile and amphibian species.

Herpetoculturist – A person who keeps and breeds reptiles in captivity.

Herpetologist – A person who studies ectothermic animals, sometimes also used for those who keeps reptiles.

Herpetology – The study of reptiles and amphibians.

Hide Box – A furnishing within a reptile cage that gives the animal a secure place to hide.

Hots – Venomous.

Husbandry – The daily care of a pet reptile.

Hygrometer – Used to measure humidity.

Impaction – A blockage in the digestive tract due to the swallowing of an object that cannot be digested or broken down.

Incubate – Maintaining eggs in conditions favorable for development and hatching.

Interstitial – The skin between scales.

Intromission – Also mating; when the male's hemipenis is inserted into the cloaca of the female.

Juvenile – Not yet adult; not of breedable age.

LTC – Long Term Captive; or one that has been in captivity for more than six months.

MBD – Metabolic Bone Disease; occurs when reptiles lack sufficient calcium in their diet.

Morph – Color pattern

Musking – Secretion of a foul smelling liquid from its vent as a defense mechanism.

Oviparous – Egg-bearing.

Ovoviviparous – Eggs are retained inside the female's body until they hatch.

Pinkie – Newborn rodent.

Pip – The act of a hatchling snake to cut its way out of the egg using a special egg tooth.

PK – Pre-killed; a term used when live rodents are not fed to a snake.

Popping – The process by which the sex is determined among hatchlings.

Probing – The process by which the sex is determined among adults.

Regurgitation – Also Regurge; occurs when a snake regurgitates or brings out a half-digested meal.

R.I. – Respiratory Infection; common condition among reptiles kept in poor conditions.

Serpentine Locomotion – The manner in which snakes move.

Sloughing – Shedding.

Sub-adult – Juvenile.

Substrate – The material lining the bottom of a reptile enclosure.

Stat – Short for Thermostat

Tag – Slang for a bite or being bitten

Terrarium – A reptile enclosure.

Thermo-regulation – The process by which cold-blooded animals regulate their body temperature by moving from hot to cold surroundings.

Vent – Cloaca

Vivarium – Glass-fronted enclosure

Viviparous – Gives birth to live young.

WC – Wild Caught.

Weaner – A sub-adult rodent.

WF – Wild Farmed; refers to the collection of a pregnant female whose eggs or young were hatched or born in captivity.

Yearling – A year old.

Zoonosis – A disease that can be passed from animal to man.

Index

C

D

E

F

M

N

O

P

R

S

T

U

V

W

Y

Photo Credits

References

Burmese Python - American Museum of Natural History
https://www.amnh.org/exhibitions/lizards-and-snakes-
alive/snakes/a-world-of-snakes/burmese-python/

Burmese Python – SeaWorld.org
https://seaworld.org/Animal-Info/Animal-
Bytes/Reptiles/Burmese-Python

Burmese Python – Wikipedia.org
https://en.wikipedia.org/wiki/Burmese_python

Burmese Python – National Geographic
https://www.nationalgeographic.com/animals/reptiles/b/bur
mese-python/

Burmese Python - National Geographic Kids
https://kids.nationalgeographic.com/animals/burmese-
python/#burmese-python-tree.jpg

Burmese Python – SnakeType.com
http://www.snaketype.com/burmese-python/

Burmese Python As Pets – The Spruce
https://www.thespruce.com/burmese-pythons-as-pets-
1237322

Burmese Python Care Sheet – Reptiles Magazine
http://www.reptilesmagazine.com/Care-
Sheets/Snakes/Burmese-Python/

Burmese Python Diseases – Mom.me
http://animals.mom.me/burmese-python-diseases-1401.html

Burmese Python: Python bivittatus – Snake – Facts.com
https://snake-facts.weebly.com/burmese-python.html

Choosing a Burmese Python – Petplace.com
https://www.petplace.com/article/reptiles/general/choosing-
a-burmese-python/

How to Clean a Snake Cage Quickly and Easily –
ReptileKnowledge.com
http://www.reptileknowledge.com/news/how-to-clean-a-
snake-cage-quickly-and-easily/

Invasive Species: Burmese Python (Life Cycle &
Reproduction) – Burmese Python
https://burmesepython.weebly.com/life-cycle-and-
reproduction.html

Snake Health 101 – Reptiles Magazine
http://www.reptilesmagazine.com/Snakes/Snake-Health-
101/

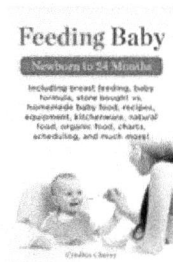

Feeding Baby
Cynthia Cherry
978-1941070000

Axolotl
Lolly Brown
978-0989658430

Dysautonomia, POTS
Syndrome
Frederick Earlstein
978-0989658485

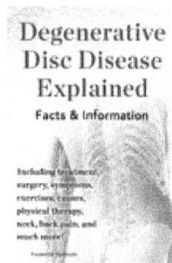

Degenerative Disc
Disease Explained
Frederick Earlstein
978-0989658485

Sinusitis, Hay Fever,
Allergic Rhinitis Explained
Frederick Earlstein
978-1941070024

Wicca
Riley Star
978-1941070130

Zombie Apocalypse
Rex Cutty
978-1941070154

Capybara
Lolly Brown
978-1941070062

Eels As Pets
Lolly Brown
978-1941070167

Scabies and Lice Explained
Frederick Earlstein
978-1941070017

Saltwater Fish As Pets
Lolly Brown
978-0989658461

Torticollis Explained
Frederick Earlstein
978-1941070055

Kennel Cough
Lolly Brown
978-0989658409

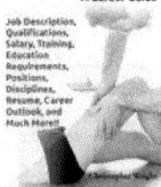

Physiotherapist, Physical
Therapist
Christopher Wright
978-0989658492

Rats, Mice, and Dormice
As Pets
Lolly Brown
978-1941070079

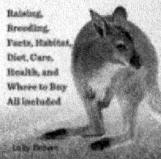

Wallaby and Wallaroo Care
Lolly Brown
978-1941070031

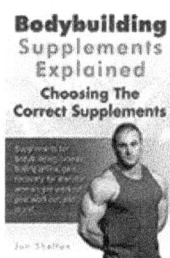

Bodybuilding Supplements
Explained
Jon Shelton
978-1941070239

Demonology
Riley Star
978-19401070314

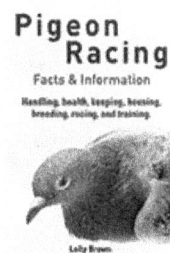

Pigeon Racing
Lolly Brown
978-1941070307

Dwarf Hamster
Lolly Brown
978-1941070390

Cryptozoology
Rex Cutty
978-1941070406

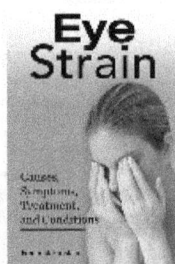

Eye Strain
Frederick Earlstein
978-1941070369

Inez The Miniature Elephant
Asher Ray
978-1941070353

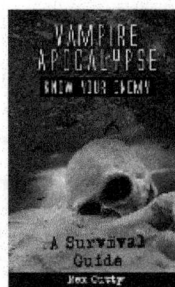

Vampire Apocalypse
Rex Cutty
978-1941070321